Tao Te Ching

Tao Te Ching

Lao-Tse

KALPAZ

ISBN: 978-93-5128-494-9(PB)

First Published in 1868
Indian Reprint in 2017

Published by

Kalpaz Publications
C-30, Satyawati Nagar,
Delhi – 110052
E-mail: kalpaz@hotmail.com
Website: kalpazpublications.com
Ph.: +91-9212142040

Chapter One

Tao (The Way) that can be spoken of is not the Constant Tao'
The name that can be named is not a Constant Name.
Nameless, is the origin of Heaven and Earth;
The named is the Mother of all things.
Thus, the constant void enables one to observe the true essence.
The constant being enables one to see the outward manifestations.
These two come paired from the same origin.
But when the essence is manifested,
It has a different name.
This same origin is called "The Profound Mystery."
As profound the mystery as It can be,
It is the Gate to the essence of all life.

Chapter Two

As soon as beauty is known by the world as beautiful, it becomes ugly.
As soon as virtue is being known as something good, it becomes evil.
Therefore being and non-being give birth to each other.
Difficult and easy accomplish each other.
Long and short form each other.
High and low distinguish each other.
Sound and tone harmonize each other
Before and after follow each other as a sequence.
Realizing this, the saint performs effortlessly according to the natural Way without personal desire, and practices the wordless teaching thru one's deeds.
The saint inspires the vitality of all lives, without holding back.
He nurtures all beings with no wish to take possession of.
He devotes all his energy but has no intention to hold on to the merit.
When success is achieved, he seeks no recognition.
Because he does not claim for the credit, hence shall not lose it.

Chapter Three

By not adoring the worthy, people will not fall into dispute.

By not valuing the hard to get objects, people will not become robbers.

By not seeing the desires of lust, one's heart will not be confused.

Therefore the governing of the saint is to empty one's mind, substantiate one's virtue, weaken one's worldly ambition and strengthen one's essence.

He lets the people to be innocent of worldly knowledge and desire, and keeps the clever ones from making trouble with their wits.

Acts naturally without desire, then everything will be accomplished in its natural order.

Chapter Four

Tao (The Way) can be infused into the nature and put to use without being exhausted.

It is so deep and subtle like an abyss that is the origin of all things.

It is complete and perfect as a wholeness that can

Round off sharp edges;

Resolve confusion;

Harmonize with the glory;

Act in unity with the lowliness.

Tao is so profound and yet in invisible, It exists in everywhere and anywhere.

I don not know whose Son It is, It existed before heaven and earth.

Chapter Five

Nature nurtures all things with the wholeness of complete virtue.

It shows the greatest and perfect kindness by giving life to let all things grow and accomplish them with the hastening of harvest.

Therefore, according to ancient custom, nature may seem unkind to regard all beings as a traditional straw dog for sacrifice.

And likewise with a saint, he may seem unkind to regard people as a traditional straw dog for sacrifice.

The space between heaven and earth is like the bellows, it appears empty yet it gives a supply that never fails;

The more it moves, the more it brings forth.

Many words lead to exhaustion.

It is better to center on the true essence within.

Chapter Six

Spirit of the valley is immortal.
It is called the mystic nature.
The gate o f the mystic nature is regarded as the root of the universe.
It is everlasting and cannot be consumed.

Chapter Seven

Heaven is everlasting and earth is enduring.

The reason that they are everlasting is because they do not exist for themselves.

Hence, they are long lived.

Thus, although the saint puts himself last, finds himself in the lead.

Although he is not self-concerned, finds himself accomplished.

It is because he is not focused on self-interests and hence can fulfill his true nature.

Chapter Eight

A person of great virtue is like the flowing water.
Water benefits all things and contends not with them.
It puts itself in a place that no one wishes to be and thus is closest to Tao.
A virtuous person is like water which adapts itself to the perfect place.
His mind is like the deep water that is calm and peaceful.
His heart is kind like water that benefits all.
His words are sincere like the constant flow of water.
His governing is natural without desire which is like the softness of water that penetrates through hard rocks.
His work is of talent like the free flow of water.
His movement is of right timing like water that flows smoothly.
A virtuous person never forces his way and hence will not make faults.

Chapter Nine

Those who overly pride wealth is like the overflowing water which shall cause damages. It is better to restrain early.

Those who are not content with fame is like polishing the edge of a knife.

The sharper it gets, the easier it is to break.

Wealth and treasures are but illusions that one cannot possess.

Those who are arrogant of their wealth and fame shall invite blame upon oneself.

The nature Tao teaches one to retreat after one's success and not to hold on to the credit.

Chapter Ten

Can one unite the body and the spirit as one and embrace the "Oneness" without departing from the great Tao? .

Can one achieve harmony with such gentleness by holding on to the true spirit within as if the innocence of an infant?

Can one free oneself from worldly knowledge and cleanse one's mind, so that no faults shall be made?

Can a ruler love his people by governing with the natural Way without personal intention?

Can the mystic gate to all life essence be opened or closed without the virtue of the mysterious nature?

Can one gain the insight of nature and become a wise person without the effort of action?

The mysterious nature creates and nurtures all things without the desire to possess them.

It performs with all efforts without claiming for credit.

It flourishes all beings without the intention to take control of.

Such is the "Mystic Te" or "Mystic Virtue."

Chapter Eleven

Thirty spokes unite around one hub to make a wheel.
It is the presence of the empty space that gives the function of a vehicle.
Clay is molded into a vessel. It is the empty space that gives the function of a vessel.
Doors and windows are chisel out to make a room.
It is the empty space in the room that gives its function.
Therefore, something substantial can be beneficial.
While the emptiness of void is what can be utilized.

Chapter Twelve

The five colors can blind one's eyes.
The five tones can deafen one's ears.
The five flavors can dull one's taste buds.
The pursuit of pleasures can derange one's mind.
The hard-to-get valuables can distort one's behavior.
Therefore, a saint cultivates himself with virtues and does not indulge himself in sensory pleasures.
He rejects those outer temptations and chooses this True Nature.

Chapter Thirteen

Honor and disgrace can surprise a person.
The greatest distress lies in one's physical body.
What does it men by "Honor and disgrace can surprise someone?"
Honor is inferior, because one who wins the favor is afraid of losing it.
And one who loses the favor is frightened with distress.
This is the significance of "Honor and disgrace can surprise someone."
What does it mean by "The greatest distress lies in one's body?"
We have fear because we worry about our physical self.
If one's body does not exist, how can one has fear?
Therefore, he who values the world as much as he values himself, can be entrusted with the ruling of the world.
He who loves the world as much as he loves himself, can be entrusted with the guidance of the world.

Chapter Fourteen

What cannot be seen is called the invisible.
What cannot be heard is called the inaudible.
What cannot be touched is called the intangible.
These three cannot be examined and comprehended.
And hence are mixed together as one.
This "Oneness" is not much brighter in the sky, as It is not much dimmer on earth.
It is not more glorious in a saint as It is not more fainter in an ordinary person.
It is everlasting and cannot be named.
It is the original void of "non-being."
This "Oneness" is the Tao which is invisible, and formless.
It may be regarded as vague and intangible.
When the Oneness Tao comes forward, Its front cannot be seen.
When one tries to follow It, one cannot see Its rear.
By abiding with the original Tao, one can master the presence.
He who knows this "Origin," shall know the teaching and principle of the Great Tao.

Chapter Fifteen

The ancient Tao cultivators were subtle and mysterious.

They were of immeasurable profundity.

Because they were too subtle to be known, so reluctantly they were being described as follow:

Cautious, as if crossing an icy river.

Hesitant, as if fearful of the surroundings.

Reverent, like an honorable guest.

Dispersed, like winter ice began to melt in spring.

Simple and sincere, like a genuine virgin.

Open-minded, like an empty valley.

Harmonized, like the turbid water.

How can one turn the turbid water into clarity?

A person of Tao would maintain peace in order to achieve pureness of the mind.

And therefore shall not be disturbed by the worldly desires.

After achieving pureness of the mind, how can one let it be everlasting?

A person of Tao would unify and harmonize himself with all beings which shall lead to eternity.

Those who abide by this Tao will not indulge themselves in the desire of greed.

It is because of this humbleness that enables one to embrace the original "Oneness," the Great Tao.

Chapter Sixteen

Human must achieve the ultimate void and maintain calmness with sincerity in order to observe the growth and flourish of all beings.

It is in this way that one can understand the law of nature.

All things and beings will eventually return to the original source.

This is called "peace."

"Peace" means returning to one's original nature.

This original nature is the eternal law. To know the nature's law is to be enlightened.

He who is ignorant of the nature's law shall act recklessly, and thus will invite misfortune.

To know the constant law of nature is to be generous.

Being generous, one is impartial.

Being impartial, one is the sovereign.

Sovereign is the nature itself.

Nature is Tao. Tao is everlasting.

When one's physical body dies away, Tao still long endures.

Chapter Seventeen

In early ancient mankind, Tao has been in existence in one's true nature.

Men possess It without knowing.

One then acts with virtue and honor which is inferior to Tao.

The less superior is to act with fear.

And the least superior is to act with disgrace.

This occurs because one does not have enough faith, and hence has no confidence.

The nature of Tao is distinguished by wordless teaching with the natural act of virtue without action.

As such, people would act effortlessly and harmonize with the Nature Tao.

Chapter Eighteen

When Great Tao declines, virtue of humanity and righteousness shall arise.
When knowledge and intelligence appear, great hypocrisy shall arise.
When the six various family relationships are not in harmony, filial piety and compassion shall arise.
When a country is in chaos, the loyal officials shall appear.

Chapter Nineteen

Transcend the saint's teaching and conceal one's wisdom for potential use, shall benefit the people a hundred fold.

Extend kindness to its ultimate and then polish to refine one's righteousness shall help the people or regain filial piety and compassion.

Employ one's subtle true nature with exquisiteness and extend one's personal benefit to share with others, shall eliminate robbers and thieves.

These three statements are apparent superficial and not sufficient to express the natural "Way" of the great Tao.

Hence, this is what people should do:

Return to their original true self and embrace the pure "Oneness."

Refrain selfness and diminish worldly desires.

Chapter Twenty

Enlightenment of the absolute Tao can free a person from worries and sorrow.

How much is the difference between a respectful response and an angry response?

How great is the difference between good and evil?

What people naturally fear, one should also fear.

One's endless desire can result in negligence of the true nature of life.

People like to pursue after excitement as if they were ascending the terrace in spring and celebrate a sacrificial feast.

But I alone remain quiet and calm like an infant who is pure and innocent.

And I alone appeared to be lost like one who has nowhere to go.

All people have a surplus, but I alone was simple and left out like a fool.

People seemed bright and shrewd, while I seemed dull.

People like to dispute, while I alone remain quiet.

I am calm and peaceful like the boundless ocean.

I am open-hearted and free like the wind blowing high above the sky without hindrance.

Everyone thinks of themselves as capable and outstanding while I appeared unlearned.

I am the only one to be different from others for I value highly the Great Tao and joyfully act accordingly.

Chapter Twenty-one

A man of great virtue is one who follows the nature way of Tao.
This Tao is vague and intangible.
Yet, in the vague and void, there is image, there is substance.
Within the profound intangible, there is essence;
This essence is genuine.
In It lies the great faith.
Since the beginning of the world, Tao has been in existence.
Only through It that one can understand the origin of all beings.
How do I know that this is the true essence?
It is through this natural Way.

Chapter Twenty-two

To yield is to preserve the whole.
To be misjudged is to be straightened.
To be hollow is to be filled.
To be battered is to be renewed.
To be in need is to possess.
To be abundant is to be confused.
Therefore, the saint embraces the "Oneness" as a standard for the world.
The wise one is not prejudiced, hence he is enlightened.
The wise one is not self-opinioned, hence he is outstanding.
The wise one does not boast of himself, hence he shall receive the credit.
The wise one does not praise his own deeds, hence can long endure.
Because the wise one does not conflict with others and therefore the world cannot contend against him.
It is not true as the ancients say, "To yield is to preserve the whole?"
Thus the "Oneness" will be honored to him.

Chapter Twenty-three

Words that cannot be heard of are natural.
A gale can not blow for the whole morning.
A rainstorm cannot last for the whole day.
What caused these effects?
Heaven and earth.
Even the actions of nature do not last long.
How much more can human's behavior last when digressed from the natural Tao?
Thus, one who follows the Great Tao,
When Tao is present, he will benefit the world with Tao.
When Te is present, he will benefit the world with Te.
When Tao and Te are both lost, he identifies himself with the people and benefits them with the enlightenment of teaching.
One who identifies with Tao is glad to be with Tao.
One who identifies with Te is glad to be with Te.
One who identifies with the loss of Tao and Te is glad to be with the lost.
If one does not have enough faith in "Tao," how can he assist others to practice with faith?

Chapter Twenty-four

He who raises himself on tiptoe cannot stand firm.
He who walks with strides cannot travel far.
He who is self-opinioned shall not be enlightened.
He who is prejudiced shall not be recognized.
He who brags about himself shall not receive credit.
He who is arrogant shall not make improvements.
In view of Tao, people who are self-centered are like the surplus food and redundant actions in everyday life.
All things disgust them.
Therefore a person of Tao will not conduct himself in such manner.

Chapter Twenty-five

Something is formed in the chaos, which existed before heaven and earth.
It is quiet and profound.
It stands alone and alters not.
It revolves eternally without exhaustion.
It is regarded as the Mother of all beings.
I do not know Its name, except to call It Tao.
When forced to give It a name, I would call It "the Great."
The Great is far-reaching.
Far-reaching is infinite.
Infinite is to return to the self-sufficient origin.
Therefore, Tao is great, heaven is great, earth is great, and so is the true-self.
There are four greatness in the universe, and true-self is one of them.
Man models the Way of earth;
Earth models the Way of heaven;
Heaven models the Way of Tao;
Tao models the Way of nature.

Chapter Twenty-six

The heavy is the fundamental of the light. Tranquility is the master of agitation.

Therefore, the saint always conducts himself with the essence of Tao and never departs from It.

Although he is surrounded by the splendor of wealth, he remains to live a simple and ordinary life.

How can a ruler govern a nation without recklessness if he indulges in power and desire?

He who acts recklessly shall lose the essence of Tao.

He who is agitated with lust and desires shall lose his true nature.

Chapter Twenty-seven

Good deeds leave no signs.

Good words leave no flaws.

Good scheme needs no deliberate plans.

A good lock uses no bolts, yet it cannot be opened.

A good knot uses no rope, yet it cannot be united.

Hence, a saint is always kind by saving other people and rejects no one.

He is always kind by saving all things and therefore nothing is being rejected.

This is the true enlightenment.

Thus, a kind person is the teacher of the unkind.

An unkind person is a lesson for the kind to learn.

He who does not value his teacher and dislikes the valuable lesson, although knowledgeable, is in fact greatly confused.

This is the fundamental essence.

Chapter Twenty-eight

To know the strong masculine principle, yet abide by the gentle female principle is like being the valley of the world where all rivers will flow into.

This is alike all virtue which will merge into the subtle Tao.

Being a valley of the world and not depart from the true nature, once can return to original pureness like an infant.

When one knows the white that is splendor, yet holds on to the black that is humble and lowly.

He can be a standard of the world.

Being a standard of the world and not deviate from true nature, one is able to return to the void of Tao.

To know what is honor, yet abide by the dishonored, is like a valley of the world which is modest and humble.

Being the valley of the world makes possible the true virtue to be complete and sufficient.

And hence can return to simplicity.

When the nature of simplicity is being manifested, it results into various vessels.

And by applying the pure simplicity, a saint can master all things.

Hence, the Great Tao is a unified Oneness which cannot be separated apart.

Chapter Twenty-nine

He who wishes to take control of the world and acts upon it,
I can see that he will not succeed.
For the world is a divine vessel,
It cannot be acted upon as one wish.
He who acts on it fails.
He who holds on to it loses.
Therefore some things move forward while some follow behind.
Some try to warm with exhaled air while some try to blow it cold.
Some are strong while some are weak.
Some are successfully accomplished while some are declined and failed.
Thus, the saint avoids all extremes, extravagance, and pride.

Chapter Thirty

One who assists the ruler with the principle of Tao,
Will not use the force of arms to conquer the world.
For such affairs will result in cause and effect.
Wherever the armies touch the land, it is turned into a wasteland of thorns and brambles.
After a war is fought, bad years are sure to follow.
Therefore, one who follows the true nature will understand the principle of cause and effect and shall not rely upon the strength of force.
By knowing the effect, thus one will not brag.
By knowing the effect, thus one will not boast.
By knowing the effect, thus one will not become arrogant.
By knowing the effect, although one has no choice, one still abides with the principle of cause and effect and does not resolve into force.
When things reach their prime, they start to age and decline.
This is the life that is diminishing and shall not reach the ultimate essence.

Chapter Thirty-one

Weapons of war are instruments of disaster.
They are rejected by all beings.
Thus a person of Tao will not dwell upon them.
According to the ancient custom of Ying and Yang,
A man of virtue values the left which is represented by Yang.
And a man of war values the right which is represented by Ying.
Weapons are instruments of evil, and are not valued by a man of virtue.
They are only used as the last resort to attain peach when all else have failed.
If their use is necessary, it is best to employ with calmness and tranquility.
Even it if means victory, it is not something pleasant.
Those who rejoice over the victory, enjoy killing.
He who delights in killing will not be favored by the people and shall not bring harmony to the world.
It is the ancient custom to favor happy events to the left as represented by yang.
While on sad occasions, it is favored to the right as represented by Ying.
When this rite is applied in the army,
The lieutenant general takes the place of the left,
And the commander-in-chief takes the place of the right.
This indicates that war is treated as if it is a funeral service;
For many lives had been killed and hence should be mourned with sorrow.
Therefore, although a victory was won,
It is treated like funeral rite.

Chapter Thirty-two

The universal Tao has no name.
Although It appears in the plainest and may seem small,
It is inferior to nothing.
If the kings and marquises can abide by the Great Tao,
All beings shall act as guests and submit to them.
Heaven and earth will then be in harmony and shall descend sweet dew.
People will not require command and orders,
Yet can treat each other equally with peace.
When Tao is manifested, names were given for the purpose of distinction.
But one must know how to attain the original pureness in order to avoid danger and disaster.
Tao exists in the universe like the rivers and streams that lead to the ocean.

Chapter Thirty-three

One who knows other people is wise.
One who knows himself is enlightened.
To overcome others is strong.
To overcome oneself is the will of power.
One who is contented is rich.
One who is determined has the strength of will.
Those who embrace their true nature shall long live.
He who is enlightened with the original nature,
Although dies physically, is eternally united with the everlasting Tao.

Chapter Thirty-four

The great Tao is ever present.
It can adjust Itself to everything.
All things live by It, and It does not deny them.
When Its work is accomplished, It does not claim possession.
It gives great love to nurture all things and all lives, but dominates not.
The true void of Tao has no desires and may seem small.
Yet all things entrust their lives to It and It does not act as their master.
This may be recognized as "the Great."
Because a saint does not restrict himself with the greatness,
Hence his greatness is accomplished.

Chapter Thirty-five

He who embraces the Great Tao shall be the guidance of the world.
By following him, the world will not be harmed and will be rendered with peace and harmony.
Pleasures and delicacy can only attract passers-by to stay temporarily.
The teaching of Tao is plain without extraordinary appearances.
It can not be seen,
It can not be heard,
It can not be depleted or exhausted.

Chapter Thirty-six

It desire shall conceal true self,
True self will manifest itself even more.
If desire shall weaken true self,
True self will strengthen itself even more.
If desire shall abandon true self,
True self will prosperous even more.
If desire shall deprive true self,
True self will give even more.
This is known as the enlightened nature that is subtle yet profound.
Gentleness overcomes strength, and the meek overcomes the strong.
Just as fish live in deep water and cannot survive after being taken out of the depths.
And the powerful weapons of a country should not be displayed,
Just like one's true nature cannot be revealed to be seen.

Chapter Thirty-seven

The everlasting Tao acts according to the natural Way.
Therefore there is nothing that It will not accomplish.
If kings and the nobilities can abide by their true nature and follow the great Tao,
All things shall be reformed naturally.
If during the process of reform, desires arouse.
I shall overcome with the simplicity of original nature.
With the simplicity of true nature, there shall be no desire.
Without desire, one's original nature will be at peace.
And the world will naturally be in accord with the right Way.

Chapter Thirty-eight

A man of superior virtue is not conscious of being virtuous, hence is truly virtuous.

A man of inferior virtue performs for the purpose of virtue, hence he is not virtuous.

A man of superior virtue acts without action, and performs with his true nature.

A man of inferior virtue acts with intentional effort.

A man of superior kindness acts a natural act.

A man of superior justice acts with righteousness and feelings for others.

A man of superior etiquette acts according to his true self, hence no one responds to him by moving away.

There, when Tai is lost, there is Te (virtue).

When Te is lost, there is humanity.

When humanity is lost, there is justice.

When justice is lost, there is etiquette.

Etiquette becomes prevalent when people fail to be sincere and honest.

Hence, chaos begins.

A person of knowledge and self-opinion will be hindered from the enlightenment of Tao.

Thus, this is the beginning of ignorance!

Therefore, one who cultivates himself with Tao,

Embraces the original nature and indulges not in sensual nature.

He abides by the fundamental Oneness and indulges not in sensory pleasures.

Thus, abandon those desires and abide by this true essence of Tao.

Chapter Thirty-nine

In the beginning, there were those who attained the Oneness;

Heaven, by attaining the Oneness became clear;

Earth, by attaining the Oneness became peaceful;

Spirit, by attaining the Oneness became divine;

True nature is like an empty valley, and by attaining the Oneness,

It became fully productive.

All things, by attaining the Oneness became alive.

Emperors and nobilities, by attaining Oneness can bring peace and prosperity to the world.

All these are the results of achieving Oneness.

Heaven, without clarity would crack.

Earth, without peace would quake.

Spirit, without divinity would be powerless.

True nature, without productivity would result in exhaustion of life.

All things, without life essence would perish.

Emperors, without Oneness to exalt them to nobility, would stumble and fall.

Thus, honor is based on humbleness.

The high builds its foundation upon the low.

Therefore, the kings and nobles call themselves "the solitude," "the unworthy," and "the virtueless."

Is this not the reason why they base their honor upon humbleness?

Hence, the highly honored do not regard themselves as nobles and have no wish to be selfcentered to think nobly of themselves as a piece of jade nor to think lowly of others as a lump of stone.

Chapter Forty

When Tao is in action, one's worldly nature can be reversed to the true nature.
Gentleness is the way of application of Tao.
All things in the world originate from the manifestation of Tao,
The manifestation of Tao is the form of being,
Which originates from the non-being of the void, the Great Tao.

Chapter Forty-one

When a superior man heard of Tao,
He cultivates himself diligently.
When an average man heard of Tao,
He is doubtful, vague and would give up halfway.
When an inferior man heard of Tao,
He laughs and thinks of It as foolish.
If Tao is not being laughed at,
It is not the Great Tao.
Thus, there is a traditional saying of,
One who is enlightened with Tao may appear foolish.
He who is advancing in Tao may appear to withdraw.
Great Tao is plain and simple which can adapt to all circumstances, although It may seem uneven and rough.
A man of superior virtue is like an empty, receptive valley.
A man of innocence may appear to be disgraced.
A man of great virtue appears to be deficient.
A man who practices Tao and actively achieves great merits may appear gentle and meek.
A man who follows his true self may appear to be changeable.
Generosity has no rough angels.
Great achievement is time consuming, and is slow to complete.
Great tone has no sound.
Great Tao is formless,
It is invisible and has no name.
It benefits all and fulfills all.

Chapter Forty-two

Tao gives birth to one.
One gives birth to two.
Two gives birth to three.
Three gives birth to all things and all beings.
All beings bear the negative physical form which is represented by Ying, and embrace the positive true nature which is represented by Yang.
With the union of these two, they arrive at a state of harmony.
Men dislike to be "the solitude," "the unworthy," and "the virtueless,"
Yet the Lords and nobles call themselves these names.
Hence, things are benefited by being humble, and damaged by profiting.
What the ancients had taught, I shall also teach as such:
A man of violence who is in disharmony between Ying and Yang that is the physical body and true self, shall die of an unnatural death.
This is the essential of my teaching.

Chapter Forty-three

The softest of all things can overcome the hardest of all things.

Regardless of being or the non-being, they all have to return to the empty void to express their gentleness.

Thus, I have learned the benefits of natural actions without personal desires.

Very few can understand the value of wordless teaching and due act of natural Way.

Chapter Forty-four

Fame and life, which one is of intimacy?
Life and wealth, which one is of importance?
To gain one but to lose the other, which is of harm?
Therefore, if one's desires are great, one would result in exhaustion.
Overstock shall result in heavy loss.
He who is contented will not suffer disgrace.
He who knows his true nature will not incur danger.
It is in this Way that one can long endure.

Chapter Forty-five

Great achievement appears to be inadequate, yet its use is never exhausted.
Great fullness appears to be void, yet its use is boundless.
Great honesty may seem to be accused of wrong doing.
Great mastery appears to be clumsy.
Great eloquence may seem to be inarticulate.
Movement can overcome chill.
Tranquility can overcome heat.
Peace and calmness is the Way to guide the world.

Chapter Forty-six

When the world lives in accord with Tao,
Fine walking horses can be retired form plowing the field.
When the world fails to live in accord with Tao,
Even pregnant mares are used as war horses,
And were forced to breed in the battlefield.
The greatest crime is to have too much desire.
The greatest disaster is not to find contentment.
The greatest mistake is to desire for endless possession.
Hence, when one is gratified with self-contentment,
True contentment can then long endure.

Chapter Forty-seven

Tao exists in one's own true self.
It cannot be found outside of one's true nature.
Hence, there is no need to leave the house to take journey in order to know the world.
There is no need to look outside of the window to see the nature of Tao.
The further one departs from Tao, the less one will be able to know.
Therefore a saint is wise to know without seeking for It.
He is wise to understand without seeing It.
He is wise to accomplish according to the Natural Way.

Chapter Forty-eight

In pursuing knowledge, one learns with intellect and desires.
Therefore one's knowledge is accumulated day after day.
In pursuing Tao, one is enlightened with the true nature and thus diminishes daily one's worldly desires and knowledge.
The continuous depletion of one's desires persists until one acts accordingly to the natural Way.
By acting without personal intention enables one to accomplish all things.
Therefore, to rule over the world,
One must act naturally without personal desires.
If one pursues with extreme effort, one shall fail to rule the world.

Chapter Forty-nine

The saint has no set mind,
He regards the wish of the people as his own wish.
He is kind to the kind, he is also kind to the unkind.
This is the true virtue of kindness.
The saint trusts those who are trustworthy.
He also trusts those who are not trustworthy.
This is the true virtue of trust.
The saint conducts himself in the world by harmonizing with all beings to be at one.
The worldly people thus look up to him attentively with their eyes and ears.
And the saint treats the people like a loving mother who loves her children unconditionally.

Chapter Fifty

Men enter this world with life and leave this world with death.

Those who work hard for living and longevity are comprised of one-third of the people.

Those who are leading their life towards death are comprised of another one-third.

Those who live with indulgence in passion and desires shall harm their life and invite death.

This is comprised of the final one-third of the people.

Why is this so?

It is because men are over-concerned with pleasures of life and hence exhaust themselves with hard work of desires of greed.

The wise one who knows how to nourish life with the Nature Tao,

When he travels, will not encounter fierce animals such as wild buffalos and tigers.

When he is engaged in the battlefield, will not be harmed by the weapons.

The horns of the wild buffalos are powerless against him.

The claws of the tigers are useless against him.

The weapons are of no avail towards him.

Why is this so?

It is because the wise one follows the great Tao and cultivates himself accordingly.

Hence, a man of Tao will not perish.

Chapter Fifty-one

Tao gives birth to all things.
And Te (virtue) nurtures them.
Matter shapes them.
The natural environment matures them.
Therefore, all things abide by Tao and honor Te.
Although Tao deserves reverence and Te deserves honor,
They are not demanded by decree,
But is a result of the Nature Way.
Hence, Tao gives life to all beings and Te nurtures, grows, fosters, develops, matures, supports, and protects them.
Tao gives birth to life and yet claims no possession.
It gives support without holding on to the merit.
It matures them but does not take control of.
This is called the Mystic Te.

Chapter Fifty-two

The beginning of the universe is Tao,
It is the mother of all.
By knowing the Mother, we will know her creations.
By knowing the creation of all lives, one can then return to the origin and abide by the Mother.
It is in this way that although the body dies, the spiritual nature will not perish.
To abide by the Mother of Tao is to keep guard on one's sensory desire and shut the doors of temptation so as to prevent one from pursuing outwards.
Thus, by doing so one's whole life may be preserved from exhaustion and pains.
However, if on the contrary one indulges oneself in the pleasure of desire and opens the door of temptation to pursue outwards,
Then one's true nature will be lost and hence is beyond rescuing.
Those who are aware of the essence of the original nature are said to be enlightened.
Those who abide by the gentleness of Tao are said to be strong.
Those who employ the glory of Tao,
And were able to return to the true nature, are ensured of no distress and is said to embrace the Nature Tao.

Chapter Fifty-three

If I were to have the very slight insight,
I would live in accordance with the Great Tao.
My only fear is, to go astray from Tao while spreading it.
Great Tao is smooth and plain, yet people prefer the devious bypaths.
Hence, the government is corrupted with luxury and splendor.
The people were exhausted with labor and left the fields to be wasted and the granaries depleted.
Under such practices, the officials would wear fine clothes,
Carry sharp swords and indulge themselves in good food and drinks.
They crave with greed to possess great wealth.
Such is said to commit the crime of robbery and certainly is not the Way of Tao.

Chapter Fifty-four

One who cultivates himself with Tao,
Firmly establishes his virtue.
He holds on faithfully to the Great Oneness,
And is honored for generations ever after.
Cultivate oneself with the Oneness, Tao and the virtue is genuine.
Cultivate a family with the Oneness, Tao and the virtue is in surplus.
Cultivate an entire village with the Oneness, Tao and the virtue is enduring.
Cultivate a whole nation with the Oneness, Tao and the virtue is luxuriant.
Cultivate the whole world with the Oneness, Tao and the virtue is universal.
Hence, by cultivating oneself, thus gains insight into one's true virtue.
By cultivating a family, thus gains insight into a loving family.
By cultivating a village, thus gains insight into a harmonious village.
By cultivating a nation, thus gains insight into the extensive benefits for the people.
By cultivating the whole world, thus gains insight into the universal peace that embrace all beings.
How do I know that the world is so?
It is through this Way.

Chapter Fifty-five

One who preserves Te (virtue) in fullness,
Is to be compared to an innocent infant.
Hence, no poisonous insects will sting him.
No wild beasts will attack him.
No birds of prey will pounce upon him.
In governing one's life, learn from an infant as such:
Its bones are soft, its tendons are tender, yet its grip is firm.
No knowing the unity of male and female,
Yet the infant's sexual organ is aroused.
This is because its life essence is pure and complete.
Crying all day, yet the infant's voice does not turn hoarse.
Such is the perfect harmony.
To know harmony is called "Everlasting."
To know everlasting is called "Enlightenment."
To overprotect one's life is called "Ill omen."
To let one's mind follow the emotional impulse is called "Compulsion."
When things reach their prime they start to age and decline.
This is the life that is diminishing, which shall not reach the ultimate essence.

Chapter Fifty-six

The wise does not speak.
He who speaks is not wise.
Keep silent and close one's mouth.
Keep guard on one's sensory organs.
Round off one's edges.
Untie the entangled.
Harmonize with the glory.
Mix with the lowliness.
This is called the Mystic Unity.
Because the wise is unified with all and has no distinction,
Thus, one cannot get close to him,
Nor can one keep far away from him,
One cannot benefit him,
Nor can one harm him,
One cannot honor him,
Nor can one disgrace him.
Therefore, he is honored by the whole world.

Chapter Fifty-seven

Govern a nation with the right principle,
Fight a battle with the tactics of surprise,
Rule over the world with peace and natural effort.
How do I know that this so?
By the following:
The more prohibitions that are imposed on people,
The poorer the people become.
The more sharp weapons the people possess,
The greater is the chaos in the country.
The more clever and crafty the people become,
The more unusual affairs occur.
The more laws and regulations that exist,
The more thieves and brigands appear.
Hence, the saint declares:
I act effortlessly with the Way of Tao,
Thus, people transform themselves naturally.
I love tranquility and peach,
Thus, people naturally follow the right Way.
I do not exhaust people with labor,
Thus, people naturally are wealthy.
I have no personal desires,
Thus, people naturally are innocent and simple.

Chapter Fifty-eight

When the government is dull,
People are simple and sincere.
When the government is complex and stringent,
People are cunning and shall cause trouble.
Calamity is what blessings depend upon.
In blessings there hides the calamity.
Who knows the ultimate end of the cycle of calamity and blessings?
Is there no true principle that exists?
The normal may revert and become unusual.
The good may revert and turn into evil.
Long indeed, man has been under such delusion.
Therefore, the saint abides by firm principle and does not depart from it.
He is honest and not mean.
He is upright and not rue.
He is honored and not eminent.

Chapter Fifty-nine

In governing one's life and serving the nature,
There is nothing better than to follow the Way of simplicity.
Simplicity is to restrain one's desires.
To restrain one's desires is to practice the virtue of Nature Way.
By practicing the virtue of Nature Way,
One is capable to accomplish anything.
With the ability to accomplish anything,
One can achieve the infinite realm.
By achieving the infinite realm,
One can then become a true leader of a nation.
To govern a nation with the Law of Nature is to be long enduring.
This is regarded as a profound and firm foundation of the everlasting Tao.

Chapter Sixty

Ruling a great nation is like frying small fish.
When they are over stirred, they will break into pieces.
Guide the world with Tao,
Then the spiritual beings would lose their power.
It is in fact not that the spiritual beings had lost their power,
But that their spiritual power cannot harm people,
But that the true nature of the saint has harmonized with the spiritual power and hence will cause no harm.
Since they both do not harm each other,
Therefore they will harmonize with the true virtue to embrace the Oneness, Tao.

Chapter Sixty-one

A great nation rules by placing itself in a lowly position like the rivers that flow into the low regions of ocean.
Hence, people will naturally be faithful to their country.
Mother nature always stays calm and quiet to overcome the unrest.
It takes the lowly position to be in peace.
Thus, if a great nation can lower itself to deal with a smaller nation,
Then it shall win the heart of the people.
And the smaller nation will willingly merge with the great nation.
And if the smaller nation can lower itself to deal with the great nation,
Then it shall win the trust and be accommodated as a part of the great nation.
Therefore, be it to take a lowly position to win over or to take a lowly position to be accommodated;
The great nation only wishes to unite and shelter all the people,
While the small nation only wishes to be a part of the nation to serve it.
Now that both are granted with what they wish for,
It is only natural for the "Great" to put itself in a lowly position.

Chapter Sixty-two

Tao is the wonder of all creations.
It is a treasure for those who are kind.
It can also protect those who are not kind.
Words of Tao can benefit all people.
Its action can guide people to follow the right Way.
Those who have gone astray, the all-forgiving Tao will not abandon them.
Therefore, it is better to embrace this precious Tao than to be crowned as kings or appointed as ministers or to possess wealth and fine horses.
So why did the ancients value and honor this Tao?
It is because "Those who seek will attain, those who offended will be forgiven."
Thus, It is the greatest honor in the world.

Chapter Sixty-three

Act without personal desire.

Manage without intentional concern.

Taste without desire of the flavor.

Hold the same regard for big or small, abundant or little and reward the unkind with kindness.

Plan for the difficult while it is easy.

Act upon the great from the beginning of the minute.

All difficult affairs must be taken care of when they are easy.

All great accomplishments must be performed from the small tasks.

Hence, a saint does not strive to do something great.

And as a result he is able to accomplish the great.

He who makes promises easily seldom keeps his words.

He who constantly regards things as easy shall result in difficulty.

Therefore, the saint is aware of the difficulties ahead and hence is cautious in managing affairs while they are sill easy and small to prevent resulting into problems.

Chapter Sixty-four

It is easy to preserve when things are stable.
It is easy to plan ahead when things have no yet occurred.
If one waits until the affair has begun,
Then the situation is as brittle as ice that easily cracks and is fragile that easily shatters.
Take actions before things occur.
Manage before things get out of order.
A huge tree grows from a tiny sprout;
A nine-story high terrace is built from heaps of earth.
A journey of thousand miles begins from the first step.
He who acts with desire shall fail.
He who tries to possess shall lose.
Therefore, the saint acts without effort and so he does not fail.
He is not eager to possess and so he does not lose.
Most people fail when they are near completion.
If one can be cautious from beginning to end, then he will not fail.
Thus a saint pursues what people do not pursue.
He does not value the hard-to-get objects.
He learns what people do not learn and avoids the faults in order to restore his true nature.
He follows the course of nature to benefit all things and dares not go astray from the right Way, Tao.

Chapter Sixty-five

The ancient Tao cultivators,
Did not lead people to acquire knowledge to be tricky,
But to guide them to restore their simplicity and innocence.
The reason people are difficult to be governed is because they are clever and witty.
Therefore, he who rules a nation with tactics and wits shall do harm to the country.
He who does not rule with such is the nation's blessing.
To know these two principles is to know the rule of nature.
To know the rule of nature is called Mystic Te (Mystic Virtue).
Mystic Te is profound and far-reaching.
It can guide all things to return to their original nature,
And thus great harmony can be achieved.

Chapter Sixty-six

The reason that river and ocean can be the Lords of all valley is because they are located in the lowly position.

Therefore, the saint humbles himself to serve all people.

And he leads the people by putting himself last for the sake of the people's welfare.

Thus, although he rules above the people,

The people do not feel him as a burden.

Although he leads in front of the people,

The people do not feel him as a threat.

Hence, the world supports him with no objection.

This is because he does not contend,

Therefore, he is above all competition.

Chapter Sixty-seven

The whole world says the Tao that I have attained is so great that It seems unreal.
Because It is indeed so great, thus It seemed unreal.
If It were real, It would have been insignificantly small.
I have Three Treasures that I hold and guard.
The first is Kindness.
The second is Simplicity.
The third is Humbleness.
With Kindness, one can be courageous.
With Simplicity, one can be generous.
With Humbleness, one can be the lead to provide guidance.
Now, if one abandons kindness and yet tries to be courageous,
If one abandons simplicity and yet tries to be generous.
If one abandons humbleness and yet tries to lead as guidance,
He is doomed to perish.
One who fights a battle with kindness shall win.
One who keeps guard with kindness shall secure.
Even the great nature shall save him and protect him with kindness.

Chapter Sixty-eight

A faithful Tao cultivator does not use force.
A good warrior does not lose his temper.
A great conqueror does not challenge others.
A good leader is humble.
This is called the virtue of peace with no contention.
This is also regarded as competence to make good use of the effort of people.
Such is regarded as achieving harmony with nature.
Such is the perfect Oneness of true nature.

Chapter Sixty-nine

In warfare, there is a saying of such strategy:
I would rather take a defensive position than to make an initial offensive move.
I would rather withdraw a foot than to march forward one inch.
Such is called to advance without advancement;
To defeat without arm force;
To fight as if there were no enemy;
To carry weapons as if there were no weapons and thus no need for the use of weapons.
There is no greater disaster than to underestimate the enemy.
To do so may cost one to lose his valuable life.
Therefore, when two armies engage in a battle,
The party that feels the sorrow of killing shall win.

Chapter Seventy

My words of Tao is easy to understand and to practice.
However, the world can neither understand nor practice them.
In my words of Tao, there is the subtle truth.
In my deeds, there is the Way of Tao.
Because people do not understand these,
Therefore they do not understand me.
Those who know me are few.
Hence, the essence of Tao appears to be more honorable and precious.
Thus, a saint may dress in ordinary coarse clothing,
Yet has a heart of gem with the true essence within.

Chapter Seventy-one

One who knows what people do not know,
Is a person of enlightenment.
One who pretends to know what he is ignorant of, is at fault.
He who is aware of what he does not know, shall not be at fault.
Therefore, a saint is flawless for he is aware of what he truly knows and what he knows not, hence he is flawless.

Chapter Seventy-two

When people do not respect the authority,
There shall be great misfortune.
Do not interfere with the people's livelihood.
Do not despise their living.
Because there is no detest against the people,
Therefore the people do not detest against the authority.
The saint realizes his true nature and hence
Does not distinguish himself.
He has a sense of self-respect and thus does not exalt himself.
Therefore, he rejects those that are self-distinguished and self-exalted.
And abides by these that are self-awareness and self-respect.

Chapter Seventy-three

He who is brave in being daring, acts recklessly and shall be killed.
He who is brave but acts cautiously and kindly shall live.
Of these two, one is beneficial while the other is harmful.
What nature wishes, who may know what the reasons are?
Thus, the saint is aware of the subtlety and profoundness of the Nature's Way,
So he takes great caution in practicing It.
The Tao of Nature,
Does not contend, yet easily wins.
Does not speak, yet always responds.
Does not summon, yet all things gather.
Does not contemplate as if at ease,
Yet all plans were devised perfectly.
The Law of Nature is like a giant web,
Although sparsely meshed, nothing can slip through.

Chapter Seventy-four

When people do not fear death,
There is no use trying to threaten them with death.
If people value their lives, and those who break the law were being executed,
Then who would dare to commit criminal act?
The life and death of all beings are handled by the executioner of Nature.
Those who substitute the nature executioner to kill,
Is like replacing the master carpenter to chop the wood.
One who substitutes the master carpenter to chop the wood,
Rarely does not hurt his hands.

Chapter Seventy-five

People starved because the ruler taxed too heavily.
People are difficult to be ruled,
Because the ruler governs with personal desire and establishes too many laws to confuse the people.
Therefore the people are difficult to be ruled.
People take death lightly,
Because the ruler pursues after luxurious life and depletes the people.
Therefore the people take death lightly.
One who does not value his life with self-desire, truly cherishes his life.

Chapter Seventy-six

When a man is alive, he is soft and supple.
When he dies, the body becomes hard and stiff.
When a plant is alive, it is soft and flexible.
When it is dead, it becomes dry and brittle.
Therefore, hard and rigid shall lead to death.
Soft and gentle shall lead to life.
Thus, a strong army with rigid force shall not win.
A thick and big tree will be cut down for its use.
The big and strong will take an inferior position.
The soft and gentle will take superior position.

Chapter Seventy-seven

The Tao of Nature is like stretching a bow.
When the stretch is too high, it needs to be pressed down.
When the stretch is too low, it needs to be raised high.
The excess will be reduced.
The deficient will be replenished.
The Tao of Nature is to reduce the excessive and to replenish the insufficient.
The Tao of man, however is otherwise.
It takes from the needy to serve those who already have a surplus.
Who can spare one's surplus to serve the world?
A person of Tao.
Thus, a saint acts without holding on to the achievements.
He accomplishes but does not claim for credit.
He has no desire to distinguish himself.

Chapter Seventy-eight

There is nothing in this world that is softer and meeker than water.
Even those that can conquer the strong and hard,
Are still not superior than water.
Nothing can substitute it.
Hence, what is soft can overcome the strong.
What is gentle can overcome the strength.
This is known by the world.
However, people cannot put it into practice.
Therefore, the saint said as follow:
He who can take the disgrace of a nation,
Is said to be the master of the nation.
He who can bear the misfortune of a nation,
Is said to be the ruler of the world.
Truthful words may seem to be the reverse of worldly practices.

Chapter Seventy-nine

When a great resentment has resulted,
Even if one tries to reconcile and make peace,
There is bound to leave some remaining resentment.
Thus, how can this be considered as a good settlement?
Therefore, a saint cultivates himself with introspection and self-discipline without blaming others for faults.
This is like the ancient custom which acts by holding on to the left part of the tally as a debtor that demands nothing from others.
Hence, a person of virtue acts as if he were the debtor.
And a person without virtue acts as if he were the creditor that demands only from others.
The Tao of Nature is impersonal which makes no exception to anyone.
It always assists those that are kind and virtuous.

Chapter Eighty

An ideal nation is small and with few people.

Although there are abundant weapons, there is no need for the use.

Let the people cherish their life and not pursue after fame and wealth,

So that they have no intention to move to faraway places.

Although there are boats and carriages, no one will ride them.

Although there are weapons and armors, there is no occasion to display them.

Let the people return to the ancient simple life where knotting ropes were used to record every event.

People would then enjoy the simple food, simple clothing, and be contented with a simple life.

And they shall live happily with the traditional customs.

Neighbors of the nations overlook one another in the near distance.

The barks of dogs and crowing of cocks can be heard.

Yet people are so contented that they enjoy their life without ever visiting each other.

Chapter Eighty-one

Words of truth are not pleasing.
Pleasing words are not truthful.
The wise one does not argue.
He who argues is not wise.
A wise man of Tao knows the subtle truth,
And may not be learned.
A learned person is knowledgeable but may not know the subtle truth of Tao.
A saint does not possess and accumulate surplus for personal desire.
The more he helps others, the richer his life becomes.
The more he gives to others, the more he gets in return.
The Tao of Nature benefits and does not harm.
The Way of a saint is to act naturally without contention.